TARA LIPINSKI

QUEEN OF THE ICE

BY BILL GUTMAN

Millbrook Sports World
The Millbrook Press
Brookfield, Connecticut

Cover photographs courtesy of Allsport (© Doug Pensinger); Liaison Agency (©William R. Sallaz)

Photographs courtesy of SportsChrome (Rob Tringali, Jr.): pp. 3, 42; Allsport: pp. 4 (© Gary M. Prior), 20 (© Doug Pensinger), 24 (© Jon Ferrey), 31 (© Jamie Squire), 44 (© Jamie Squire); Liaison Agency: pp. 11 (© Lawrence Schwartzwald), 36 (© Evan Agostini), 39 (© Karin Cooper), 41 (© Karin Cooper); St. Louis Post-Dispatch: p. 13; Reuters: pp. 16 (Mike Blake/Archive Photos), 27 (Blake Sell/Archive Photos), 32 (Blake Sell/Archive Photos); AP/ Wide World Photos: p. 21; Agence France Presse/Corbis-Bettmann: p. 28; © Jim Malucci/Outline: p. 46

Library of Congress Cataloging-in-Publication Data
Gutman, Bill.
Tara Lipinski : queen of the ice / Bill Gutman.
p.   cm. — (Millbrook sports world)
Includes bibliographical references (p.) and index.
Summary: A biography of the fifteen-year-old figure skater who became the youngest gold medal winner at the Olympics in 1998.
ISBN 0-7613-1456-3 (lib. bdg.). — ISBN 0-7613-1287-0 (pbk.)
1. Lipinski, Tara (1982–   )—Juvenile literature. 2. Skaters—United States—Biography—Juvenile literature. [1. Lipinski, Tara, 1982–   . 2. Ice skaters. 3. Women—Biography.] I. Title. II. Title: Queen of the ice. III. Series.
GV850.L56G88 1999
796.91'2'092—dc21
[B] 99-17740 CIP AC

Published by The Millbrook Press, Inc.
2 Old New Milford Road
Brookfield, Connecticut 06804
www.millbrookpress.com

TARA
LIPINSKI

Tara Lipinski arrived at Nagano, Japan, in February 1998 prepared to enjoy herself fully. After all, there aren't many 15-year-olds who have the chance to compete in the Winter Olympic Games. But Tara was a world-class athlete who was expected to take home a medal in figure skating. She wasn't favored to win the gold—her United States teammate, Michelle Kwan, was the top choice of most experts—but that didn't bother Tara. She viewed the entire Olympic experience with joyful enthusiasm, and, by the time she was ready to skate, she simply wanted to do her best. After the first day of competition, Michelle Kwan had the lead, with Tara second. Unless she fell during the long program of the second day, it was almost guaranteed that Kwan would retain her lead and win the gold.

Indeed, she did skate well, though her program was conservative. She didn't take chances or do many difficult maneuvers. But her scores seemed good enough

Tara's superb performance in the ladies' free skate at the 1998 Winter Olympics earned her an excellent score for technical merit. Combined with her score for artistic impression, it was enough to let her win the gold medal over Michelle Kwan, who was favored to take first place.

to hold off the competition. Finally, it was Tara's turn. Though no one her age had ever won a gold medal in the Winter Olympics, Tara came out on the ice with a confident smile that never left her face.

Once she began to skate, the audience quickly sensed that it was witnessing something special. Tara whirled, jumped, turned, and leaped around the ice, a picture of spirit and joy. The judges knew what was happening. Tara was performing the most technically difficult program in women's Olympic figure-skating history. And she was doing it almost perfectly.

When she performed the very difficult triple-loop, triple-loop combination jump without a flaw, the audience roared, and Tara's smile became even wider.

The triple-loop combination was totally hers. No other female skater had ever tried it at the Olympics. When she finished, she had successfully performed seven triple jumps, including a second triple-triple. And when the scores were posted, everyone knew what had happened. Tara Lipinski had pulled off an incredible upset. She had vaulted past Michelle Kwan into first place and had won the gold medal! She was an Olympic champion at the age of 15.

One writer called her performance "the most glorious of the Olympics, a stunning, spirited long program that snatched the gold medal for women's figure skating from favorite Michelle Kwan."

Tara exuded the enthusiasm and excitement of her youth. "I went out there and had a great time," she said. "I didn't think about winning. I didn't think about beating anybody. I didn't want to come off the ice disappointed. I was so relieved to skate a great program under a lot of pressure. Doing it at the Olympics is just so emotional.

"I would have stayed out there all night if I could. I'm just going to walk around enjoying being Olympic champion."

BORN TO SKATE

Tara Lipinski and skating were almost always a perfect fit. Tara was born June 10, 1982, in Philadelphia, Pennsylvania. She was the first and only child of Pat and Jack Lipinski. She was named after the plantation, Tara, in the classic movie *Gone With the Wind*. Her mother and father had seen that film on one of their first dates, and Pat Lipinski felt that was a special way to remember. "I told Jack that if we ever had a little girl I was going to name her Tara," she said.

Tara was an active child from the start. Once she took her first steps, it seemed that walking just wasn't enough. She began to roller-skate at the age of 3 and not only learned fast but was also apparently fearless. Soon her parents began taking her to age-group competitions, and she excelled. At the age of 5, she won her first championship, a regional roller-skating title in New Jersey, where the family was living at the time.

When she was just 6, Tara asked her father to build a little platform that she pretended was an Olympic podium. Dreams sometimes begin very early. She continued to roller-skate and, not surprisingly, soon discovered another kind of skating. Once she saw how fast ice skaters could move, she asked her parents to take her to an ice rink.

"When she took her first turn on the ice she was flopping around pretty good," her father recalled.

Feeling they might be making their daughter nervous by watching her, Pat and Jack Lipinski went inside for a cup of hot chocolate. When they returned to the rink, Tara was skating around as if she were still on her roller skates. She was a natural. Not only was she good at ice skating, but she soon began to love it.

Before long, two things happened that would change Tara's life. First, she began taking skating lessons. The lessons soon showed her parents, coaches, and Tara herself how good she could be. And second, the family moved from New Jersey to the Houston suburb of Sugar Land, Texas.

At first, Tara settled in to what seemed like a normal lifestyle in Sugar Land. She made new friends and joined the fourth grade class at Highlands Elementary School. Her father had a job as an executive with an oil company, and her mother worked as a secretary. All three were happy in Sugar Land, the place that Tara considers her hometown.

She also continued her skating lessons, practicing whenever she could. There had to be some adjustments to the so-called normal lifestyle, however. For her parents, it meant taking Tara to her skating lessons at some strange hours.

Tara and her mother would rise at around 3 A.M. so Tara could take her lessons before school. She would often eat her breakfast on a tray in the backseat of the car. This kind of schedule is not uncommon for young people who participate seriously in individual sports. Lessons and practice sessions make up a busy schedule for both the youngsters and their parents. But Tara practiced willingly and was soon becoming an outstanding young skater.

"There were times back then when I had to make choices," Tara said. "If I received an invitation to a friend's birthday party and it meant missing skating time, I would skip the party."

This routine continued for two years. Then in June 1993, the family had to make a huge decision. Both of her parents knew that Tara had a special talent for skating. Even at the age of 11, Tara had begun talking about competing in the Olympics. Everyone knew that to advance to that level, she would need professional coaching. And she couldn't get that in Sugar Land.

Finally, the Lipinskis came to a decision. Tara's mother would give up her job and take Tara back east, to Wilmington, Delaware, where she would begin working under Coach Jeff DeGregorio. Her father would stay in Sugar Land, working at his job, maintaining their home, and taking care of their four dogs. He would fly east on weekends to visit his family. It would be a significant change for all of them.

"It's a sacrifice for Jack and [me] not to be living together," Mrs. Lipinski said. "But you do all you can for your child. Both Jack and I love Tara very much, and we wanted to give her a chance to pursue her dream."

"Tara is our only daughter, and we wanted to support her," Jack Lipinski added. "We tried to interest her in other sports. We bought her a horse. She took tennis lessons and played basketball. But she was so small that basketball just wasn't in the cards."

Once her parents decided that they were willing to make the sacrifice, they told their daughter to think it over carefully. She, too, would be sacrificing by giving up what is usually considered a normal childhood.

"It was pretty much my decision," Tara said, looking back at her choice to move to Delaware. "[Skating] was just what I loved to do, and I wanted to go as far as I could. I really did believe. I never thought about the odds. I never even thought that in the whole rink only one person could become world champion."

So Tara and her mother left Texas for Delaware. Once there, Tara would receive constant coaching and train, practice, and just about live for ice skating. She would continue school with a team of three tutors. She could adjust to that. The tough part was that their close-knit family would be separated. But when asked later if she regretted missing much of a conventional childhood, she said, "No, I have no regrets at all. I wouldn't change what I did for anything. All the hard work, everything. I missed some things with my friends, but that's okay. The biggest sacrifice was living away from my dad. That was difficult."

It wouldn't be long, however, before Tara's hard work and sacrifice began showing results.

A FIGURE-SKATING TRADITION

Figure skating has always been one of the most popular sports at the Winter Olympics. Competitions began on an international level in 1882, with the first world championships held in 1896. The sport became an Olympic attraction the first time it was a medal event in 1908. To become world-class with a chance at an Olympic medal, skaters must work extremely hard.

Today, there are still two phases to Olympic competition—the short and long programs. The short program counts for one-third of the skater's total score. It consists of eight required moves or elements: three jumps, three spins, and two fast-step sequences of footwork. Among the moves are a double or triple jump, and a jump combination, which can include a double and triple jump, or two triple jumps. These must be done without a step in between. The triple jump is the most difficult jump to execute well.

Required moves in the short program are judged with two marks: one for how well the required elements are performed (the technical), and a second mark for presentation (the artistic). Together, these marks evaluate the overall program. Skaters may perform the moves in any sequence within a time limit of 2 minutes and 40 seconds. And they may select their own music.

The long, or free-skating, program counts for two-thirds of the total score for the competition. There are no required elements during the 4-minute 30-second time limit for men, and a 4-minute limit for women. Skaters can also select their music for this program. They incorporate into their programs as

Women's figure skating has always captured a wide audience, but its popularity has dramatically increased in recent years. In this picture, taken at the Rockefeller Center ice rink in New York City, are the present and past of the sport: Tara Lipinksi and Jo Jo Starbuck, a two-time Olympian.

many difficult spins, jumps, and other moves, and as much footwork, as they can. The object is to show all their technical and artistic skills.

Skaters are encouraged to show their creativity, change the pace of the performance, and display innovative moves. Judges look at the difficulty of the moves and jumps, and how well they are executed. As with the short program, there are two sets of marks: the first for technical merit, the second for overall presentation or artistry. A 6.0 is a perfect score. A 5.9, 5.8, or 5.7 is also considered very good. Scores from the judges are added and averaged.

Over the years, skaters have become more athletic. Today they are able to jump higher than ever before and are trying more difficult maneuvers and combinations of jumps and spins. This makes it harder than ever before to become a world-class figure skater and to compete with the best. The sport, however, is more popular than it has ever been. Besides national and world championships and the Olympics, there are many professional ice shows, exhibitions, and professional competitions. Many of these are shown on television.

At the Olympics, medals are given for both men and women, as well as pairs skating and ice dancing by pairs. But often, it is the women's individual champion who emerges as the darling of the Olympics. Many of the gold-medal-winning women have gone on to become celebrities in their own countries and around the ice-skating world.

Tara was the youngest athlete ever to win a gold medal at the U.S. Olympic Festival. At the competition in July 1994, she was just a month past her 12th birthday.

When a young girl like Tara Lipinski begins skating seriously, it isn't long before an Olympic gold medal changes from a dream to a goal. But not many young skaters ever reach the stage where they can seriously contend for a spot on the Olympic team. Only a special few can do that.

THE MAKING OF A CHAMPION

Once Tara began getting professional coaching, her progress was amazing. In 1994, when she was not yet 12 years old, Tara began competing for the first time. She was still in the Novice Division, but she was going up against the best skaters in her age group, and she dominated them.

Despite her tiny size, which made her look wisplike on the ice, Tara already had a huge heart. She loved competition and always went out to skate her best. Her delicate appearance may have given her competition a false sense of security. They soon learned that this little girl could skate like a tiger.

In 1994 she took first place in the Blue Swords Novice competition, then won the Midwestern Novice and Southwestern Novice titles. After taking second place at the 1994 National Novice Championships, Tara competed in the U.S. Olympic Festival in St. Louis, Missouri. She was just a month past her 12th birthday when the competition, for future Olympians, began.

This time Tara dazzled everyone, putting on a showstopping performance to become the youngest athlete ever to win a gold medal at the festival. She was the toast of the town, and from that point on everyone in the skating world knew just who she was. What they didn't know was just how close she was to challenging the best in the world.

Unlike many preteens who are beginning to excel at a sport, Tara was never pushed by her parents. Consequently, there was no rebellion, no burnout. She loved to skate and to compete. She wanted to excel more than anyone. By the

1995–1996 season, it was time to step it up even more. Tara and her parents decided she would make a coaching change.

Her new coach was the well-known Richard Callaghan, who was already working with national champions Nicole Bobek and Todd Eldredge. To study with this coach, Tara and her mother had to move to Bloomfield Hills, Michigan, a suburb of Detroit. Tara would become part of the Detroit Skating Club, which would remain her home base as she rose to prominence in the skating world.

Once again she had to settle into a different kind of lifestyle. Her father would fly in from Houston on weekends whenever he could. That was the only time the family would be together, except for their yearly vacation, to Disney World in Florida. Once again, that was the hard part. Tara's everyday routine wasn't easy, either.

School was a daily four-hour tutoring session with a team of three tutors making sure that Tara stayed right at her class level. She then had four 45-minute training sessions spread out over the rest of the day at the Detroit Skating Club. In the evening, she had to do her homework and then get ready for the same routine the next day. It took discipline and commitment, but Tara seemed to have plenty of both.

She wasn't lacking anything with her tutors. Not only did they cover all the subjects, but Tara also had use of any equipment she needed for school, including a desk, books, a microscope, and a computer.

"She's got classes year-round, basically whenever time permits," said her math tutor, Jerry Kotasek. "She works very hard, she's very energetic, and she takes it very seriously."

In 1995, Tara began entering major competitions and performing well. She finished second in the United States National Junior Championships, then fourth in the World Junior Championships. She continued in junior events as the 1996

season began, finishing first or second in four major competitions. Then in the World Junior Championships she finished fifth, down one spot from her finish the year before.

But despite that, her overall performance was much better. Not yet 14 years old, and still under 5 feet (152 centimeters) in height, tiny Tara was becoming a terror on the ice. Her parents and coaches came to a decision. She would begin skating in the senior division and would enter the 1996 World Championships. It must have been an awe-inspiring event for Tara. She would be skating against the best skaters in the world.

In the short program she seemed tentative and unsure. Her performance wasn't up to the form she had so often displayed in the juniors. After the first day, Tara was in 23rd place and out of medal contention. But in the free-skating long program, she gave everyone in attendance a preview of what was to come.

A more relaxed Tara showed her athleticism and skills by landing seven triple jumps perfectly. The crowd gave her a rousing ovation. Although Tara didn't come close to medaling, she had moved up eight places after the long program to finish 15th. Afterward, she admitted that the World Championships had been a kind of strange experience.

Tara entered the world of senior competition in a big way, by competing against the best in the world in the 1996 World Championships. She finished 15th overall, which wasn't bad for a 13-year-old skater.

"My memories of the Worlds are different than I thought they'd be," Tara said. "It went so fast number one. I really was mad about that. I wanted it to take a long time, and I think I was in shock. And then it hit the next couple of days, and I was like, 'Oh, my gosh. I want to do it again.'"

The World Championships in 1996 were won by an American teenager, 15-year-old Michelle Kwan. Michelle seemed poised to be the next dominant United States figure skater. Little did anyone know that another teen, two years younger, would suddenly emerge and challenge Kwan for championship supremacy. That teen was Tara Lipinski.

AN AMAZING DOUBLE TRIUMPH

Tara's climb to the top began at the 1996 United States National Championships. Skating with poise and confidence, she surprised a lot of people by finishing in third place with the bronze medal. But that still didn't prepare the figure-skating world for what was about to happen in 1997.

During this period, Tara continued to work hard with Coach Callaghan. She and her mother still saw her father only on weekends. But Tara's work ethic showed that she appreciated her parents' sacrifice. She was obviously taking advantage of the opportunity she had been given.

Sometimes, in fact, she worked too hard. Coach Callaghan often had to slow her down. "Tara is almost too much of a perfectionist, who insists on repeating a jump 20 times without stopping," the coach said. "Part of my job is to caution her to use her body conservatively as she gets older and stronger. We haven't seen anyone with this combination of athletic ability and lyrical quality since Janet Lynn in the 1970s."

Though 14, Tara remained very small, almost tiny. She was barely 4 feet 10 (147 centimeters) and weighed between 75 and 80 pounds (34 and 36 kilograms). It was hard to believe that she was a world-class skater. Though she could rotate on her spins and turns with ease, she didn't get as high off the ice with her jumps as other skaters.

"[Coach Callaghan] wants more height," she explained, "but speed is a big thing for me. I'm tiny, so it's hard for me to get up like the bigger skaters and finish everything. The bigger skaters have more power, so they can push up higher to give them more time. For me, it's harder."

Tara wasn't airborne as long as bigger skaters, so she had less time to complete her double and triple jumps. That meant she had to make the turns quicker if she wanted to complete them before her skate touched down on the ice. Her athleticism allowed her to compensate, and when she arrived in Nashville, Tennessee, for the 1997 United States Championships, she was ready.

Michelle Kwan once again was favored to win, but this time Tara didn't fall behind in the short program. She was in striking distance of the lead. In the free-skating long program, Tara unveiled her new routine, which featured seven triple jumps, including a pair of triple loops in combination. She was the first woman to land this maneuver successfully. She came off the ice to a huge ovation, and when the scores were announced, she had become the United States champion at the age of 14!

Tara was on a roll. After the U.S. Championships, she won the Champions Series Final in Hamilton, Ontario, Canada. Now she prepared for her second World Championships, which would be held in Lausanne, Switzerland, in March 1997. If she could win it this time, she would become the youngest world champion ever. The youngest so far was the legendary Sonja Henie, who was just months older than Tara when she won her first world title back in 1927. The record had stood for 70 years.

Despite her young age, Tara had become a mentally tough competitor. She had learned just how to balance her nerves. "I realize if you have too much nerves

Tara beams after a brilliant performance at the 1997 United States Championships, which she won. Her momentum would carry her to two more major victories within the space of a month, including the World Championships.

then that will ruin [the performance]," Tara said. "I also realize that if you are too calm then you won't push as hard, and you won't have that adrenaline pumping. So I'm nervous and that's good. But I can't get too nervous, so I try to stay calm."

That might seem a little hard to understand, but Tara knew just what she was talking about. At Lausanne, Tara skated brilliantly. Once again she landed her trademark triple-triple, as well as five other clean triple jumps. And once again she finished ahead of Michelle Kwan to become the youngest world champion ever. She had done it. Some were calling it the dawn of the "Tara Era." But not everyone felt that Tara was the future of figure skating.

There was some criticism. Articles in a few European publications began referring to Tara as the "Robotic Shrimp." They were picking on her diminutive size and claiming that her program seemed technical and mechanical. She lacked, according to the publications, the artistic refinements of

Michelle Kwan and Oksana Baiul, another former teenage Olympic champion.

And one of America's top male skaters, upon seeing Tara's medal-winning free-skating program at the World Championships, said, "It was nice. It was pleasing to the eye. But it was a little girl's program."

It's unclear why Tara was being criticized. Perhaps it was hard to believe that one so young could be so good. As Tara herself had admitted, her small size prevented her from leaping as high as many others could. But the judges at both the U.S. and World Championships were seasoned veterans of figure skating. And they felt that Tara was the best.

Tara greets and signs autographs for young fans upon her victorious return from the 1997 World Championships in Lausanne, Switzerland.

She received another boost in December 1997 when she was chosen as the U.S. Olympic Committee's SportsWoman of the Year. At 15½, she was the youngest woman ever to receive the award.

"It's such a great honor," Tara said. "Of all the sports people in the U.S., I got picked. It just feels really good. I know only [two] other skaters got it, so it's a big thing for me."

PREPARING FOR THE OLYMPICS

Tara's great double 1997 triumph in the U.S. Nationals and World Champion-ships made her a serious contender for the Olympic gold medal in 1998. After all, if she was that good at 14, it seemed she could only get better. She had a superior work ethic as well as a dream to become the Olympic champion. But that didn't mean it would be easy. Michelle Kwan was also a champion and still a teenager herself. Either way, it seemed as if the United States had the two best women skaters in the world.

Besides the prestige of an Olympic gold medal, the women's figure-skat-ing champion often becomes a revered public personality and, in many cases, a celebrity. The American gold-medal winners were Tenley Albright in 1956, Carol Heiss in 1960, Peggy Fleming in 1968, Dorothy Hamill in 1976, and Kristi Yamaguchi in 1992. All went on to star in professional ice shows.

The most recent winners, beginning with Fleming, also became commercial spokespersons for various companies and found other ways to remain public fig-ures if they chose. In the media-driven commercial world, it was estimated that if an American woman won the figure-skating gold medal at the 1998 Winter Olym-pic Games at Nagano, Japan, she could be worth between $10 and $15 million.

With an Olympic year on the horizon, much was being made of a Lipinski-Kwan rivalry, but Tara quickly put to rest any rumors that there might be some animosity between the two teenage skaters.

"I don't think there is a big rivalry going on," she said. "We get along. It's so strange to hear people say that. When we go in the locker room, we talk. I don't see [the rivalry], but I guess it's going to be there. I think it is that we are both going for the same dream—the Olympics."

If Tara had an edge with her great double triumph in 1997, the momentum swung back to Kwan during the early part of the 1997–1998 season. Tara was second to Kwan in the Skate America competition, then became ill and finished second in the Trophy Lalique competition in Paris.

Then, in early 1998, she traveled to Philadelphia, the city of her birth, to defend her United States Championship. But there was more at stake than just the U.S. title. The top three finishers would also win a berth on the United States Olympic team.

Once again Tara had to call upon all her resources and mental toughness. She suffered a rare fall during the short program and after the first day of competition was in fourth place. If she didn't move up, she wouldn't even make it to the Olympics. The pressure was really on. But she skated brilliantly in the long program, hitting her triple jumps and moving up to take the silver medal.

"I think I have an inner desire to skate well," she said afterward. "When I messed up the short program, I didn't want to go out and make another mistake in the long and have people say, 'Oh, no, she's falling apart.' I wanted to go out there and show everybody I can do a great long [program] and there was really no problem."

She hadn't defended her U.S. title, but she had made the Olympic team. Michelle Kwan had skated magnificently and took first place. In fact, it was perhaps the finest performance she had ever given. She was so artistic and lyrical in her presentation that she received 15 perfect 6.0 scores out of the 36 marks in the competition, and it was said that several judges were moved to tears. Kwan was now the favorite to take the Olympic gold.

Many thought that the pressure was on Tara. She had faltered several times in major events over the past few months. But Tara remained confident.

"Coming back the way I did [in the U.S. Nationals] with all the pressure I was under gives me great confidence going into the Olympics," she said. "I know I can do anything now."

Former gold-medal-winner Carol Heiss Jenkins felt that the friendly rivalry between the two young Americans was helpful to both.

"With Tara and Michelle, this is probably the best thing," Heiss Jenkins said. "They may not know it, but it's pushing them to the maximum of their ability."

Another former gold-medal-winner, Kristi Yamaguchi, wouldn't pick a winner between the two teens but felt that Tara's great passion could be an advantage.

"Tara is a fantastic skater and mature beyond her years," Yamaguchi said. "She has a freshness. You can see the love of the sport pouring out of her. That makes it easy to enjoy her and gets an audience behind her."

Almost every story about Tara mentioned her age. Her choreographer, Sandra Bezic, felt that point was being overstated. "I don't think we should make an issue of her age," Bezic said. "It's not something we can do anything about. She's 15 and she is phenomenal."

Tara and her parents made another decision when they traveled to Japan for the Olympic Games and the competition. "We decided to let Tara live in the village [with the other athletes]," Pat Lipinski explained. "We sat her down and told her that no matter what happened, she had to enjoy having been here."

By contrast, Michelle Kwan chose to stay in California and train until three days before the skating was to begin. She missed the opening ceremonies, and

No matter the outcome, Tara always seems to have fun on the ice. Although she lost her title as U.S. champion to Michelle Kwan in 1998, Tara's second-place finish was good enough to secure her a spot on the U.S. Olympic team.

when she did arrive, stayed with her coaches outside the village. Tara, meanwhile, was enjoying everything the Olympics had to offer.

She had the memories of arriving by bus at the Olympic village, unpacking and moving into her room, and seeing the figure-skating arena, the "White Ring," for the first time. She said she would never forget marching in the opening ceremonies, meeting legendary athletes like hockey's Wayne Gretzky, and posing for a picture with a 516-pound (234-kilogram) sumo wrestler.

"If I don't get an Olympic medal, what am I left with?" she said. Then she answered her own question. "I want my Olympic memories. This is my chance to have fun."

Even her coach agreed with the decision. He was confident that Tara was mature enough, even at the tender age of 15, to make sure she took care of business. "I knew she was organized enough to go to bed on time, get up on time, and not miss the bus to practice," Richard Callaghan said. "Tara has her day structured so she's a giddy teenager [during certain] hours and a really hard worker [during other] hours."

By the time the skating competition was slated to begin, Tara was relaxed and feeling right at home. She was ready to perform. As Coach Callaghan said, "She's a little anxious to get going. But that's normal for her."

But would that be enough to give her an advantage over Michelle Kwan? Only time would tell.

OLYMPIC GOLD

The opening night of the women's skating competition quickly showed two things. The first was that Michelle Kwan and Tara Lipinski were the class of the field. The second was that Kwan looked like she was going to be the gold medalist. Tara skated well, but Kwan was absolutely outstanding.

Tara skated first, performing cleanly and confidently in the short program, showing exuberance on the ice and impressing the judges. When it was over, she seemed elated.

"Emotionally, it's the best I've ever skated the program," she said. "I felt like I wanted to cry. The triple [jump] felt great. When I landed it, I thought,

Tara was determined to make the most of her Olympic experience. Staying at the athletes' village and participating in the opening ceremonies, where she is pictured with fellow figure skater Todd Eldredge, helped her to do so.

'Everything is fine now.' I wished I could just keep going and enjoy the moment. I wished it was [time for] the long program."

Tara's marks put her in first place until Michelle Kwan hit the ice. Her short program wasn't quite the perfection she had shown at the U.S. Championships, but again she was artistically superb. As one writer put it, "Kwan is a brilliant skater, one of the most beautiful in the sport's history, and her artistry is absolutely breathtaking."

Sure enough, Kwan finished the short program in first place. Tara was now second. Both skaters had nailed each of their jumps and spins. Kwan's artistry had given her the lead, but Tara was close enough to win with a perfect performance on the second night. Most felt, however, that unless Kwan faltered and made a mistake, there was no way Tara could realistically catch her.

Tara still seemed relaxed. Although some experts said she should concentrate more on holding on to second place rather than on surpassing Kwan for first, she was still friendly and accessible. She told the media how "cool" it had been to meet Tipper Gore, wife of Vice President Al Gore, in the athletes' village. If she was nervous or tight, it didn't show.

Kwan skated first in the final elite group of six skaters. Her program was controlled, artistic, and a bit conservative. She didn't take any chances, though

Despite the excitement of being at the Olympics, Tara's coach knew that she was dedicated enough to concentrate on practicing when she needed to. Two days before the official start of the Games, Tara took a practice run at the White Ring.

she hit all seven of her triple jumps. It was a solid, if not spectacular, skate. All nine judges gave her 5.9 for artistic impression. But the marks for technical merit were a bit lower. Five judges gave her 5.7, while the four others graded her at 5.8. There was now a crack, no matter how slight, for Tara to slip through. Finally, it was Tara's turn. She was the next-to-last skater of the competition.

Tara hit the ice like a dynamo and never stopped. As her friend and training partner, Todd Eldredge, said, "She looked like she was going to burst. It was great."

Using her confidence to full advantage, she performed her toughest maneuver, the triple-loop, triple-loop combination, right in front of the judges. When she landed it cleanly, she grinned from ear to ear, then continued on to perform the most technically difficult program in Olympic history. Not only did she do it without a flaw, but she skated with a joy and passion that had everyone in the arena clapping rhythmically and riding around the rink with her. Even the sparkle of the silver sequins on her costume seemed to put the tiny 79-pound (36-kilogram) skater in a special light.

Watching from the stands, her mother thought back on all the years of work and the sacrifice that the family had made. She felt the tears welling in her eyes. "All of it went through my mind, all of it," she said. "Her ups and her downs."

When she finished her program, Tara literally ran across the ice to the center of the rink, her fists pumping enthusiastically in the air. The crowd roared as they had never done before. She then joined her coach to await the judges' marks—and to see who would win the gold.

The marks for artistic impression were six 5.8s and two 5.9s. Kwan had scored all 5.9s. But when the marks for technical merit were posted, it quickly became obvious what had happened. Tara received six 5.9s and three 5.8s. It was enough for her to pass Kwan in total score. She had won the gold in incredible fashion! It was one of the greatest upsets in Olympic history.

After the celebration with her coach, parents, and others, Tara had time to think about her great performance. "The Olympics are pretty stressful," she said. "You have a lot of pressure, but I just relaxed and let myself have fun. I think it worked. I also think when I stepped on the ice, I had a feeling I knew what the Olympics were about. I had that feeling of just pure joy, and I went out there and put it in my program."

A disappointed Michelle Kwan realized that Tara's exuberance and the technical complexities of her program had made the difference. "I enjoyed my perfor-

Pure joy is hard to hide. As her scores for the free skate came up, Tara, Coach Callaghan, and a friend realized that she had won the gold medal.

mance, but it seemed like I was in my own world. I didn't open up or really let go."

With two great skaters, the difference between first and second place is often very small. The Olympics in Nagano turned out to be Tara's stage, and *her* gold medal. But fans of both skaters hoped the rivalry would continue for years to come.

Michelle Kwan skated a beautiful but conservative program that earned her the silver medal. Tara's more difficult program earned her higher marks for technical merit, and the victory was hers. Here, both skaters show off their medals.

TURNING PRO

Tara and her parents realized that they would have to make some decisions when the Olympics ended. As everyone knew, Tara's gold-medal-winning performance could easily be translated into dollars. Top athletes can make money by endorsing products as well as performing. And Tara, at age 15, was certainly marketable.

But before making a decision, Tara and her parents returned for a huge homecoming celebration in both Houston and Sugar Land. After landing in Houston to a celebration at the airport, Tara and her family rode in a limousine to Sugar Land, where an estimated 60,000 people turned out for a parade and homecoming celebration for their Olympic heroine.

Tara was given keys to both cities, and March 1, the day of her arrival, was declared "Tara Lipinski Day." She was cheered and honored all day long.

When she spoke, Tara told the huge crowd that she was "so happy to be back home." She thanked everyone, adding, "I'll always remember this day." She also said that the only way her life had changed so far was that more people were asking for her autograph. But now she was looking forward to spending a few quiet days at home with her parents and their beloved dogs.

The final word, however, came from a former Olympic gold medalist, sprinter Mike Marsh, who was also from Sugar Land. Speaking to Tara, he said, "From this day forward, whenever you hear the national anthem, it's never going to be the same. You've inspired lots of kids. You should realize just how powerful it is—what you've done out there."

Tara now had a chance to relax and think about her future. She and her parents talked about many things. There was a time when amateur skaters were not allowed to earn any money from their sport. Those rules had changed over the years. Many amateur athletes can earn a solid living by getting appearance fees and doing endorsements. But there are still more opportunities for a professional, especially in skating. If Tara turned pro, she could no longer compete in events such as the United States and World championships. To return to the Olympics, she would have to make a special request to have her amateur status reinstated.

On the other hand, she was just 15 years old, with many years of skating ahead of her. She would be just 19 for the Winter Games in 2002. There would still be time then to become a professional. The decision wasn't an easy one. Finally, in early April, Tara was scheduled to appear on the *Today Show* from Baltimore, where she was to perform in a figure-skating show. That's when she made her surprise announcement. She told the national audience that she had decided to become a professional skater.

The major reason, she said, was that she could spend less time training and more time with her family. "I realized after Nagano how important it is to me to be with my mom and dad, be all together, have fun, and really be a family again," she said. "Now I'll have four-day weekends and be able to be with my family, because they mean so much to me. I don't want to be 21 and not know my dad.

"I've accomplished my dream," Tara added. "I think I need to give something back to them, so we can be a family again and really have that connection."

The decision made, it didn't take Tara long to begin her professional life. Her first pro event took place on April 24, a made-for-TV contest called the Skate, Rattle & Roll Figure Skating Championships in North Charleston, South Carolina. There were celebrity judges on hand, and Tara would be competing against former Olympic champions Katarina Witt and Oksana Baiul, as well as Surya Bonaly of France, who was also making her professional debut.

Not surprisingly, Tara was the star of the show. She skated two perfect routines, landing all her jumps and playing to the crowd like a seasoned veteran. She led the competition all the way, getting perfect 10s from the celebrity judges, who used a different scoring system from that of the Olympics. She was the winner, with all the performances set to be shown on national television two weeks later.

Tara's professional career had begun.

A PROFESSIONAL CELEBRITY

Even before she turned pro, Tara was signing endorsement deals. She began representing Mattel toys and Minute Maid Orange Juice. And a few months before the Olympics she had signed to work with the clothing company DKNY Kids. It was thought to be the first such deal between a figure skater and a major fashion company.

Tara would be making in-store appearances and do some print advertising. But it became apparent early on that she was not going to use her newfound celebrity status only to make money through commercial ventures. She discovered that being a celebrity gave her a special opportunity to help others.

With her Olympic triumph still fresh in everyone's mind, she was named a national spokesperson for the Boys & Girls Clubs of America. Tara joined with other luminaries such as actor Denzel Washington, retired General Colin Powell, and baseball superstar Ken Griffey, Jr., as spokespersons for the clubs. As part of her responsibility, it was announced that she would be visiting clubs throughout the United States. She would be speaking to children, giving them tickets to her skating performances, and conducting clinics wherever possible.

During a visit to the Kips Bay Boys & Girls Club in New York City, Tara seemed right at home. She intermingled with the members as they showed her their facility. She even played a video game of football against some of

the other kids, then watched an exhibition of dancing in the dance room. In the auditorium, the kids chanted, "Tara, Tara, Tara" before she was officially introduced.

"Tara is an example of exactly what the Boys & Girls Club is telling you," said Kurt Aschermann, senior vice present of marketing and communication for the clubs. "If you have a dream…you've got to work at it and go after it.… She is what the clubs are all about."

As for Tara, she told the gathering, "My skating club provided a real support system for me, and I'm not sure I could have pulled it off in Nagano without them. You have that kind of support in your club here. Everybody here is lucky to have the Boys & Girls Clubs."

Later, Tara said she hoped she could set a good example for all club members around the country. "This feels great," she said. "I hope when [the kids] look at whatever they want to do in life, they get inspired by what I've done and my being here and that they set big and great goals and achieve them."

Actively supporting the Boys & Girls Clubs was not the only public service that Tara was performing. In May 1998, she made her debut as a Washington lobbyist, promoting antitobacco legislation before Congress. Still a month away from her 16th birthday, Tara stood beside President Bill Clinton on the South Lawn of the White House to urge lawmakers to support an antismoking measure that would raise cigarette prices and curb tobacco advertising.

One of Tara's first post-Olympic projects was the publication of her book, Totally Tara. *Here she poses at a book signing in New York City with her dog, Coco.*

Tara had also agreed to be the lead voice of the Campaign for Tobacco Free Kids, a nonprofit organization that was pushing for antismoking legislation. She said that most of her friends didn't smoke because they were athletes and quite aware of the health hazards involved. "I also know a great deal about peer pressure," she added. "A lot of kids [start smoking] because they think it is cool."

Pat Lipinski, who accompanied her daughter to Washington, D.C., said that Tara had always hated smoking. "If we were in a restaurant and somebody started smoking, she couldn't handle it. It bothers her big time," her mother said.

Tara's schedule was still a busy one, but it did not include the isolated and intense training that she had done for so many years before her Olympic victory. Spare time could now be spent with her parents. If they weren't with her at a show, she would fly home and see them in Sugar Land. It was a much more relaxed way to live.

On the ice, Tara continued to be a major attraction. She became part of the Champions on Ice tour, one of several professional groups performing around the country. In August 1998, both Tara and men's gold-medal-winner Ilia Kulik of Russia (who had also turned pro) announced they were leaving the Champions on Ice tour to join the International Management Group's Stars on Ice tour.

Tara uses her celebrity status to influence lawmakers to pass legislation against one of her pet peeves: smoking. In May 1998 she joined her mother, Pat, and more than 1,000 young people for an antitobacco rally.

Her agent said that one reason for the decision was a chance to work with veteran skating star Scott Hamilton, who was possibly in his last year on tour. It was believed that Tara would have a one-year contract (plus an option) for close to $2 million a year.

"I really enjoyed [the Champions on Ice] tour," Tara said. "But this is an opportunity for me to expand and do more things. I think it will improve my skating. It's like a show, acting a little bit."

Working with a new coach, she continued to learn more about skating and developed new routines that were part of her new tour. By October she was fully immersed in Stars on Ice, a tour that had started 12 years earlier. Scott Hamilton, the founder of the tour, was just as excited as the teenage skaters. "Everybody here feeds off each other's energy," he said. "And with a lot of new people in the show, their excitement in a new environment feeds our energy level.

"With Tara, no one is more suited to this type of show. She's a very smart person with a wonderful head on her shoulders, because she's had a strong up-bringing. She has an open mind and a great level of ability. And she can't wait to get on the ice and be part of everything."

Kristi Yamaguchi, one of the stars of the tour, was also anxious to skate with Tara. "For Tara, this is a whole new world," Kristi said. "I went through something

Tara started her professional skating career with the Champions on Ice tour, but later decided to join the Stars on Ice tour, during which this picture was taken. Stars on Ice gave Tara the chance to work with veteran skating star Scott Hamilton.

similar. And it's important to this tour, because of the youthful exuberance and young blood she brings. That's something that keeps all of us going."

Tara Lipinski continues to entertain and amaze her many fans with her love of skating, her talent, her youthful zeal, and her athleticism. She's more of a pure performer now, but the competitor still burns within, and she has said that she may seek to return to Olympic competition in 2002. "The Olympics changed my whole life," she said. "At the moment I won, it was, 'It's yours forever. You don't have to give it up.' Even when I look at the medal now, it's so awesome.

"My plan was always to try to win the Olympics. Now, it's on to other things, and I don't regret any decisions. I know I've done the right things for my life."

Of course, people will always criticize, and some have said that Tara didn't have to move into the professional ranks so early. But even at her young age, she knows there is no looking back. "[The criticism] hurts you and bothers you sometimes," she said. "But you've got to be strong. It helps me to be out there with the fans. The people who were criticizing me are not in the position to understand. They have not gone through 12 years of training and living away from their dad for five years.

"The reasons for becoming a professional were obvious to me. It was the best thing for me and my family."

For Tara, that's the thing that counts the most.

Will Tara return for the 2002 Winter Olympics? Could she win another gold medal? We'll have to wait and see. Here she is pictured during her winning performance at the Champions Series Final in Ontario, Canada, in 1997.

TARA LIPINSKI: HIGHLIGHTS

1982   Born on June 10 in Philadelphia, Pennsylvania.

1987   Wins a regional roller-skating championship in New Jersey.

1989   Begins ice skating.

1991   Moves with parents to Sugar Land, Texas.

1993   Moves with mother to Wilmington, Delaware, and begins training with Coach Jeff DeGregorio.

1994   Takes first place in the Blue Swords, Midwestern, and Southwestern Novice competitions and finishes second in the National Novice Championships.

Takes the gold medal at the U.S. Olympic Festival in St. Louis, Missouri.

1995   Moves with mother to Bloomfield Hills, Michigan, and begins training with Coach Richard Callaghan at the Detroit Skating Club.

Finishes second in the National Junior Championships, and fourth in the World Juniors.

1996   Finishes fifth at the World Junior Championships, and fifteenth at the World Championships, her first senior division competition.

Wins the bronze medal at the U.S. National Championships.

1997   Wins the National Championships in Nashville, Tennessee, and the Champion Series Final in Ontario, Canada.

Travels to Lausanne, Switzerland, to become the youngest skater ever to win the gold medal at the World Championships.

Named by the U.S. Olympic Committee as its SportsWoman of the Year.

1998   Wins the gold medal at the Olympic Games in Nagano, Japan.

Announces her decision to turn pro and wins her first professional event, the Skate, Rattle & Roll Figure Skating Championships in North Charleston, South Carolina.

Becomes a national spokesperson for Boys & Girls Clubs of America.

Meets President Bill Clinton and addresses a congressional committee in support of antismoking legislation.

Joins the Champions on Ice tour. Later signs a contract with Scott Hamilton's Stars on Ice tour.

FIND OUT MORE

Gatto, Kimberly. *Michelle Kwan: Champion on Ice*. Minneapolis: Lerner, 1998.

Poynter, Margaret. *Top 10 American Women Figure Skaters*. Springfield, NJ: Enslow, 1998.

Rutledge, Rachel. *The Best of the Best in Figure Skating*. Brookfield, CT: Millbrook, 1998.

Wheeler, Jill C. *Tara Lipinski*. Minneapolis: ABDO, 1998.

Yamaguchi, Kristi. *Always Dream*. Dallas: Taylor Publishing, 1998.

How to write to Tara Lipinski:
Tara Lipinski
c/o Detroit Skating Club
888 Denison Court
Bloomfield Hills, MI 48302
Tara's Web site: www.taralipinski.com

INDEX